D1174697

Molly Pitcher

Heroine of the War for Independence

Leaders of the American Revolution

Leaders of the American Revolution

Molly Pitcher

Heroine of the War for Independence

Rachel A. Koestler-Grack

CHELSEA HOUSE
P U B L I S H E R S
A Haights Cross Communications Company ®
Philadelphia

CHELSEA HOUSE PUBLISHERS
VP, NEW PRODUCT DEVELOPMENT Sally Cheney
DIRECTOR OF PRODUCTION Kim Shinners
CREATIVE MANAGER Takeshi Takahashi
MANUFACTURING MANAGER Diann Grasse

Staff for Molly Pitcher
EXECUTIVE EDITOR Lee Marcott
EDITORIAL ASSISTANT Carla Greenberg
PRODUCTION EDITOR Bonnie Cohen
PHOTO EDITOR Sarah Bloom
COVER AND INTERIOR DESIGNER Keith Trego
LAYOUT 21st Century Publishing and Communications, Inc.

© 2006 by Chelsea House Publishers,
a subsidiary of Haights Cross Communications.
All rights reserved. Printed and bound in the United States of America.

A Haights Cross Communications ✦ Company ®

www.chelseahouse.com

First Printing

9 8 7 6 5 4 3 2 1

Library of Congress Cataloging-in-Publication Data

Koestler-Grack, Rachel A., 1973–
    Molly Pitcher: heroine of the War for Independence/Rachel A. Koestler-Grack.
        p. cm.—(Leaders of the American Revolution)
    Includes bibliographical references and index.
    ISBN 0-7910-8622-4 (hard cover)
  1. Pitcher, Molly, 1754–1832—Juvenile literature. 2. Monmouth, Battle of,
Freehold, N.J., 1778—Juvenile literature. 3. Women revolutionaries—United
States—Biography—Juvenile literature. 4. Revolutionaries—United States—
Biography—Juvenile literature. 5. United States—History—Revolution,
1775-1783—Biography—Juvenile literature. I. Title. II. Series.
    E241.M7K64 2006
    973.3'34'092—dc22
                                                                      2005004814

All links and web addresses were checked and verified to be correct at the time of publication.
Because of the dynamic nature of the web, some addresses and links may have changed since
publication and may no longer be valid.

Contents

OUR RIGHTS AND OUR LIBERTIES

Molly—
The Pitcher!

T he sweltering heat of June 28, 1778, pressed down on the American soldiers like a heavy hand. Each steamy breath seemed thicker than the last. The hot air dried their throats, and the gun smoke suffocated them. For hours, the Patriots had been fighting the British soldiers near Freehold, New Jersey, in what came to be known as the Battle of Monmouth.

On June 24, General George Washington, the commander-in-chief of the Continental Army, had called a council meeting to establish a battle strategy that might prove effective against the British troops, under the command of the British general Sir Henry Clinton. The council group agreed that the best strategy was to avoid a major confrontation with the British. After a harsh winter, some military leaders thought that the Continental Army was not yet ready for a major battle. They wanted to be cautious, even though the Continental Army was well trained, better equipped, and had almost the same number of men as the British. Instead, it was agreed that Washington would send a small number of soldiers to harass the enemy's right and left flanks, or sides of the army formation. Their mission was to burn bridges, muddy wells, and cut trees to fall across roads. Using these delaying tactics, Washington and his council hoped to slow the march of the British troops and wear them down.

Early on the morning of June 28, Washington and his Continental soldiers arrived at the nearby settlement of Englishtown. Against the council's decision, he ordered his soldiers to attack the British near Freehold.

Realizing that Washington was ignoring the council's recommendations, General Charles Lee took over as commander. General Lee was one of the council members who had argued strongly against a major battle with the British.

After a short skirmish, Lee ordered the soldiers to retreat. Furious with Lee's command, Washington took charge and led the troops back into battle. For the rest of the day, the two armies engaged in a ferocious fight.

Soldiers seemed to drop like dominoes—some from wounds, others from exhaustion. Then, in the midst of a field of dead and wounded bodies, a figure was visible. Through the smoky haze dashed a woman, not more than 24 years old. Her name was Mary Ludwig Hays. But the soldiers knew her as Molly Pitcher.

BRINGING AID

"Molly Pitcher" was not simply a nickname given to Mary Hays. It was the name given to all women in battle who carried a pitcher of water to the soldiers. In the 1700s, Molly was a common woman's name. Instead of trying to remember the name of all of the women in camp, soldiers simply called them "Molly."

Molly Pitcher gained fame for her actions during the Battle of Monmouth, when she stepped in to fire his cannon after her husband was shot.

The name "Pitcher" came from the occasion when most soldiers were calling for a woman—in the midst of battle, when they were in desperate need of a drink of water or in need of water to properly recharge their cannon. They would call out for the "pitcher" to be brought to them.

Accepting the nickname, Mary Hays willingly became Molly Pitcher. On this sultry day, Molly's job was even more important. Over the boom of cannon fire, Molly carefully listened for the cries of the Continental Army's men. "Molly! The Pitcher!" one soldier would shout. Quickly, Molly ran to his side and offered him the water.

Molly Pitcher had not chosen to provide this valuable service to the soldiers simply out of a sense of patriotism or a belief in the cause for which the Continental Army was fighting. Her husband, William Hays, was a soldier in the Continental Army. To be close to him, she followed the army, and served in whatever way she could—performing some simple nursing, helping to wash and mend clothing or prepare meals, and providing that valuable drink of water in the midst of battle.

On this day, William Hays manned a cannon as the battle raged around him. From time to time, Molly checked on William and gave him something to drink. She stood by his side and watched him clean, load, and fire his cannon.

After watching him for a while, Molly was about to turn and walk away. She had to run back through the field to see if anyone needed water. Just then, William fell to the ground. Molly spun around and dropped to her knees. Her husband had been shot. He was unconscious, but he was not dead.

AN ACT OF COURAGE

Without a moment's hesitation, Molly grabbed the cannon rammer and cleaned the barrel, just as she had watched her husband do countless times. She loaded another ball and fired.

Throughout the day, Molly continued to "swab and load" William's cannon. At one point, a cannon ball shot right between her legs. It tore a hole in her skirt, but did not hurt her.

When the fighting finally ended, late in the afternoon of June 28, 1778, the Battle of Monmouth had become the longest battle fought in the Revolutionary War. During the night, the British soldiers retreated. The Patriots claimed the victory.

The Battle of Monmouth was a critical turning point in the colonial fight for independence. It proved that the Patriots could hold their own against the well-trained British Regulars. The battle also inflicted serious losses on the British Army.

The Battle of Monmouth also marked a turning point in the geography of the Revolutionary War.

Molly Pitcher's courage during the Battle of Monmouth earned her the praise of General George Washington. News of her bravery spread through the Continental Army, inspiring other women to become more directly involved in the Revolutionary War.

Shortly after it had been fought, the battleground in the war for independence shifted to the south.

After the battle, General Washington thanked Molly for her bravery. News about Molly's actions spread throughout the Continental Army, and she became one of the best-known heroines of the American Revolution. Other women in the army camps heard her story and were often inspired to imitate her actions.

The strength and clear sense of duty that Molly Pitcher demonstrated in the Battle of Monmouth were a motivation to those women in the colonies who believed in the Patriot cause and wanted to provide some service to the fight for independence. Other women would follow Molly Pitcher, performing their own acts of bravery during the Revolutionary War. Some women offered to help the Continental Army in any way they could—as cooks, launderers, and even spies. Their contributions came at a critical time in the struggle for freedom, and helped to ensure the ultimate victory of the Continental Army.

Test Your Knowledge

1 Where was the Battle of Monmouth fought?

a. New Jersey.

b. Pennsylvania.

c. New York.

d. North Carolina.

2 Who was General Charles Lee?

a. The commander-in-chief of the Continental Army.

b. An officer in the Continental Army who ordered a retreat during the Battle of Monmouth.

c. The commander of British troops during the Battle of Monmouth.

d. Molly Pitcher's husband.

3 Why was Mary Hays known as Molly Pitcher?

a. It was a nickname given to her by her father when she was a child.

b. She had taken the name Molly Pitcher when she married.

c. She had assumed a secret identity in order to serve in the Continental Army.

d. Molly Pitcher was the name soldiers used for any woman carrying water during a battle.

4   Why was Molly Pitcher honored by General Washington after the Battle of Monmouth?

    a. For her courage in carrying water onto the battlefield.

    b. For spying on the British and providing information to the Continental Army.

    c. For taking over her husband's cannon after he was shot.

    d. None of the above.

5   Why was the Battle of Monmouth significant?

    a. The Continental Army demonstrated that they could fight against the British Regulars.

    b. The British suffered significant losses during the battle.

    c. It was one of the last major battles of the Revolutionary War fought in the north.

    d. All of the above.

ANSWERS: 1. a; 2. b; 3. d; 4. c; 5. d

OUR RIGHTS AND OUR LIBERTIES

Working Girl

I t was somewhere near the middle of the eighteenth century that Gretchen Ludwig first cradled her newborn baby girl in her arms. The exact year of birth of the woman who would become known as Molly Pitcher is not certain. It is believed to be somewhere around 1754 that Mary Hays first entered the world.

Mary was the first and only child of Gretchen and John George Ludwig. The birth of a child to the Ludwigs meant more than a simple addition to the family; it meant the arrival of a child who could, one day, help them run their farm.

The Ludwigs owned a dairy farm in New Jersey. At the time of Mary's birth, New Jersey was one of the 13 colonies belonging to Britain that stretched along the east coast of North America. The colonies were separated into three regions: the New England Colonies, the Middle Colonies, and the Southern Colonies. At the time of Mary's birth, New Jersey was part of the Middle Colonies.

The Ludwigs were immigrants who had traveled to the American colonies from Germany in 1730. Little is known about Mary's parents and ancestors. Much of their early history was lost on the journey to America. What is known is that many German immigrants traveled to the American colonies in the early part of the eighteenth century to escape the violence in their homeland. At the time, Germany was frequently under attack by armies of various nationalities. Often, entire villages were burned to the ground, and many Germans were killed or tortured. Many of the immigrants settled in the middle colonies; by 1745, about 45,000 Germans lived in Pennsylvania alone.

Much about the earliest years of Mary's life is uncertain. Even the spelling of her last name inspires debate. Because many people did not read or write, and others were immigrants who spoke little if any English, names and words were often spelled the way they sounded. Because of this, spellings often varied widely, depending upon the person recording information. Mary's family was no different, and her last name has also been recorded as "Ludewig" and "Ludwick."

A HARD LIFE

As a child, Mary Ludwig was expected to work hard, to help in the many tasks required to keep a family farm running smoothly and efficiently. In this, she was no different from other children her age. Colonial children began doing chores at the age of five or six. Mary would have been expected to help weed the garden, churn butter, gather eggs, feed and water the animals, and even milk the cows. At an early age, Mary learned how to bake bread from scratch, make soap, and sew. She was a strong and hardy girl and, as an only child, her contribution was vital in helping her parents.

Colonial children were expected to help with chores. As a small girl, Mary Ludwig baked bread, made soap, fed and watered the farm animals, and helped with sewing.

Life on the farm was difficult. In spite of the hard work, the family had little money. Mary probably received no formal education. Few schools existed in the Middle Colonies in the 1700s. Many children never went to school. They were expected to help on the farm or with the family business. Some parents taught their children how to read and write, but even this little bit of education was rare. The sons of wealthy families would attend grammar schools and then college to train them to become lawyers, doctors or clergymen. Sons whose fathers were not so wealthy—young men who would become an apprentice to an artisan, a shopkeeper, or a craftsmen—were sent to writing schools to perfect the reading and writing skills they would need in business.

But such training was not thought necessary for farm children, and certainly not for girls. In later years, Mary could not sign her own name. Instead, she used an "X" as her "mark." It is likely that she never learned to read.

HIRED HELP

When Mary was about 15 years old, a doctor's wife from Carlisle, Pennsylvania, visited the Ludwig farm. Anna Irvine watched Mary doing her chores. She thought Mary was a hard worker and was impressed by her household skills. She admired Mary's strength and pleasant, quiet manner and decided that she would make a good servant. Irvine asked Gretchen Ludwig if she could hire Mary to work for her in Carlisle.

Wealthy colonial families often hired poor immigrant girls as servants or nursemaids for their children. At 15, Mary was considered old enough to leave home and begin working.

When she was about 15, Mary Ludwig was hired by a doctor's wife as a servant and moved to Pennsylvania, a colony founded by William Penn (shown here negotiating a treaty with Native Americans) in the seventeenth century for Quakers to safely practice their religious beliefs.

Carlisle was 150 miles away from the Ludwig farm. It was a long distance in those days, and meant that the Ludwigs might never see their daughter again. Gretchen Ludwig wasn't sure if she could bear to lose her only child. But she left the decision up to Mary. She gently told Mary that she did not have to go, but that the money would help the farm.

Mary knew that her parents were poor. If she took the job, she would make money. She could then send the money home to her struggling parents. Mary must have hated to see her family suffer. She decided to help them in any way that she could. According to a friend, "She was as kind as anyone who ever lived." [1]

With tears in her eyes, Mary Ludwig gave her mother and father a hug good-bye. She climbed up onto her horse and gave her childhood home one last look. Then, she and Mrs. Irvine galloped down the long gravel driveway. Little did Mary know that this was only the beginning of a grand adventure.

BECOMING A WIFE

It took Anna and Mary more than a week to make the trip from the Ludwig farm in New Jersey to the central part of Pennsylvania, where Carlisle is located. The journey stretched through winding mountain trails. They waded through creeks and streams. All the while, Mary tried to imagine what her new home would look like.

When they arrived in Carlisle, Mary was surprised by the hustle and bustle of the town. Founded around the time of her birth, in 1751, Carlisle was a patchwork

quilt of pastures and farmhouses. Workers on the out-
skirts of the town were digging a quarry, building the
Carlisle prison. Before too long, this jail would hold
British prisoners during the Revolutionary War. The

The Colonial Town of Carlisle

When Mary Ludwig arrived in Carlisle at the age
of 15, she found herself in a town that was
vibrant with activity, quite different from the quiet
life she had known on her family's farm. Located in
south-central Pennsylvania, the town of Carlisle was
officially founded in 1751, only a few years before
Mary was born. Its history was as interesting as hers
would prove to be.

At the beginning of the eighteenth century, most
settlements in the British colonies in America clung closely
to the coastline. It was along the coastline that new
settlers arrived in America, and as the journey west was
difficult, long, and hazardous, few ventured far from
the ports where they had first entered the colonies.
While Philadelphia rapidly became one of the busiest,
largest cities in the British Empire, the lands west of
Pennsylvania's Susquehanna River (in the central part of
the colony) represented the frontier—a wilderness where
no settlers had ventured. The territory was populated by

town would also serve as a center for military action when the war began, becoming an important site for the manufacture of muskets, ramrods, and other weapons of war.

Native Americans, and colonial laws did not apply to land that far west.

All this began to change in 1736, when the family of William Penn (who had founded the colony of Pennsylvania) formally purchased land west of the Susquehanna River and opened it up for settlement. Penn had intended Pennsylvania to be a haven for those fleeing religious persecution, and he encouraged Scots-Irish immigrants to settle in Carlisle and establish a Presbyterian church there. Carlisle soon became the center of the Presbyterian faith in Pennsylvania, and a home to many new settlers.

By 1750, enough settlers had arrived in the region to spark the creation of a county, named Cumberland County. Carlisle was named the county seat one year later.

German immigrants—many from the Rhine Valley— soon followed the Scots-Irish settlers into the region. Mary might have heard German spoken in the streets and in the shops. By 1785, most of the people living in and around Carlisle were of German heritage.

But all of this was still in the future. When Mary arrived in Carlisle, she saw a thriving community, very different from the life she had known on the farm. There were shops that sold clothing and shoes. Flour mills dotted the creek shore.

Anna Irvine put her new servant to work immediately, instructing her to scrub the floors, wash the laundry, and mend the clothes. The chores were tedious, but Mary kept reminding herself of the money she could send back home.

Anna Irvine's husband was a doctor. When Dr. Irvine was not treating patients, he spent a lot of time discussing politics. One of his favorite topics was the growing conflict between colonists and the British Parliament in the colony of Massachusetts.

The conflict had begun in 1765, when a group calling itself the Sons of Liberty had been formed to protest a tax placed by the British Parliament on the colonists—a tax known as the Stamp Act. The Stamp Act placed a tax on many of the items critical for daily life in the colonies—things like newspapers, books, legal documents, diplomas, licenses, and playing cards. Parliament had passed the tax to pay for some of the debt Britain incurred as a result of the French and

Indian War, but it quickly became a symbol of unjust authority to many in the colonies.

The Sons of Liberty were the first organized symbol of resistance. Formed in Boston, the Sons of Liberty set fire to the homes of the men who enforced the hated tax, placing pressure on anyone who might cooperate with British authorities. Soon, other branches of the Sons of Liberty were formed in other colonies.

The Stamp Act was eventually repealed, but on September 30, 1768, British warships sailed into Boston's harbor, and British troops (known as Regulars) disembarked and quickly occupied the city. The residents of the colonies considered themselves British citizens, and it was with shock and disbelief that they realized that their own country was sending troops into one of their cities to march through the streets, seize homes and possessions, and threaten their fellow citizens. Resistance began to spread from Massachusetts to the other American colonies.

This was the subject of much discussion in the Irvine home. Mary Ludwig would have heard Dr. Irvine discussing these events with others, debating whether or not British troops would soon be marching through Pennsylvania streets, as well.

But news from Boston did not distract Mary for long. She had been introduced to a barber in Carlisle, a young man named William Hays. There was not much time for dating or romance. Before long, William asked Mary to marry him.

On July 24, 1769, William and Mary said their wedding vows at the Irvine home. Mary Hays thought that she was leaving domestic service to settle down to a quiet married life. However, events outside of Carlisle would soon make a quiet life impossible.

Test Your Knowledge

1 Where did Mary Ludwig grow up?

   a. In a small Quaker village in Pennsylvania.

   b. On a dairy farm in New Jersey.

   c. In the small town of Carlisle, Pennsylvania.

   d. In Boston, Massachusetts.

2 Mary Ludwig's parents were immigrants from which country?

   a. Scotland.

   b. England.

   c. Ireland.

   d. Germany.

3 When Mary Ludwig was 15, she left home to do what?

   a. To marry a farmer.

   b. To work as a seamstress.

   c. To work as a servant.

   d. To work in a shop.

4 After leaving home, where did Mary Ludwig live?

   a. Philadelphia, Pennsylvania.

   b. Monmouth, New Jersey.

   c. Carlisle, Pennsylvania.

   d. Concord, Massachusetts.

5 Who was William Hays?

a. The doctor for whom Mary Ludwig
   worked.

b. The barber who became Mary Ludwig's
   husband.

c. A leader in the Sons of Liberty in Boston.

d. None of the above.

ANSWERS: 1. b; 2. d; 3. c; 4. c; 5. b

Trouble Rises

In order to understand Mary Hays, and appreciate her history, it is important to first understand the world in which she lived. Her life reflected America at a time of transition—a period of change that marked the end of the colonial era and the beginning of a new age of independence.

During the seventeenth century, Great Britain established 13 colonies along the eastern coast of North America. These settlements were split into three regions: the Northern Colonies, the Middle Colonies, and the Southern Colonies. The New England Colonies were New Hampshire, Massachusetts, Rhode Island, and Connecticut. New York, New Jersey, Pennsylvania, and Delaware made up the Middle Colonies. The Southern Colonies consisted of Maryland, Virginia, North Carolina, South Carolina, and Georgia.

By the mid-1700s, the population of the colonies had grown dramatically. More land was needed to build towns and farms. France owned a large piece of land west of the Appalachian Mountains. Some of this land also belonged to Native American groups. Conflict quickly grew as British settlers attempted to move west into this territory. In 1754, the British went to war with France and the Native Americans to gain control of this territory in a conflict that became known as the French and Indian War (1754–1763).

The French and Indian War was the beginning of a larger war called the Seven Years War (1756–1763). The Seven Years War involved all major European powers. But to the colonists, the major conflict was the struggle against the French for control of North America. The conflict in America was tied to hard feelings left over from an earlier war—King George's War (1744–1748). In this war, the colonists had won a military victory against the French, but the terms of the peace treaty forced Britain to return the land that had been won. Hatred grew between the French and the English in America.

In 1755, France held large stretches of land in North America. The French had land claims that covered most of Canada and land following the Mississippi River all the way down to what we know today as Louisiana. When the English colonists began moving west, into French territory, the French built several forts along the frontier. One of these forts was Fort Le Boeuf, near Lake Erie. The English claimed that this land belonged to them.

To settle the matter, a young colonial soldier in the British Army, Major George Washington, set out with a group of soldiers to evict the French. The 22-year-old major led his men through the nearby woods. Along the way, they ran into a group of French scouts. Washington ordered his men to fire, killing ten French soldiers and capturing 22 others. This event occurred at a time of official peace.

The French accused Washington of killing the men in cold blood. They even tricked him into signing a document that stated his plan was to assassinate the men. The translator told Washington that he was signing a document that admitted responsibility for his attack on the scout party.

The conflict did not take long to build. The English sent a second, larger military force under the command of General Braddock into the region. As these men marched to the fort, they did not see the Native Americans and French soldiers hiding in the woods. The battle turned into a massacre of the colonists. A war between the English and the French had begun. King George officially declared war on May 15, 1756, even though fighting had actually begun in America two years earlier.

PAYING THE BILL FOR FREEDOM

By 1763, the British had won the war. But the cost of conducting the war was high, and troops still remained in the colonies to guard against further attack. The British legislature, or Parliament, turned to the colonies to help pay for these bills. Parliament placed taxes on some of the items that were shipped into the colonies from Great Britain. The British would use the money collected from the taxes to pay for the debts from the French and Indian War.

The import taxes enraged the colonists. Many colonists believed that they should decide what taxes the colonies had to pay. There were no colonial representatives in Parliament. Therefore, the colonists had no control over the laws that were passed to govern them. They felt it was wrong to have taxation without representation. Others believed that the colonies should have a government of their own.

In 1765, Parliament passed the Stamp Act. This law required colonists to pay tax on every piece of printed paper they used. Ship's papers, legal documents, licenses, newspapers, and even playing cards were taxed. The money raised would pay for British troops, who were stationed along the Appalachian Mountains to protect the colonies from possible Native American attacks.

The cost of the tax was small, but the colonists again disagreed with it. They thought these taxes would lead to greater, more troublesome taxes. If they did not speak up now, Parliament might begin to tax everything. In protest, some colonists refused to buy the goods. A year later, Great Britain removed the tax because of the boycott.

In 1767, Parliament passed yet another tax, this time on import items such as glass, lead, paint, paper, and tea. These laws were called the Townshend Acts. Again, colonists boycotted British goods to protest the taxes. Tensions rose in the colonies. British soldiers stood guard in some cities, like Boston, to keep peace.

TROUBLE IN BOSTON

Trouble was bound to break out. On the snowy night of March 5, 1770, a few boys threw snowballs at each other as they ran down Boston's darkened streets. They noticed a few British soldiers standing at their guard post. The boys decided to have some fun with them. They hurled their snowballs at the British soldiers. They continued throwing snow-balls, enjoying the fact that the soldiers did not seem to react.

Before long, other passersby gathered around the boys. They joined in the battle, too. Soon, the streets

Conflict with British rule began in Boston with the Boston Massacre; engravings like this one were used to gain support for the protests against unjust taxation.

were crowded with men and boys, all throwing snow and ice at the small cluster of British soldiers.

The British guards felt outnumbered. Many of the snowballs were sharp and heavy with ice. Then, the crowd started shouting insults and chanting. The soldiers feared that the mob might attack them.

One soldier fired a shot, then another. Suddenly, the guards began firing randomly into the mob. The streets erupted into a brawl. Bostonians used any weapon they could find—knives, sticks, and fists—to attack the British soldiers.

When the streets finally quieted, five colonists were dead. American newspapers heralded that a "massacre" had taken place in Boston. Writers used this term to convince people that British soldiers in the colonies meant trouble. Some people wanted colonists to think that it would be dangerous to stay under British rule.

Finally, Great Britain again lifted the taxes. Parliament removed the tax on every item except tea. At this time, tea was a staple beverage, much like coffee today. The British believed colonists would rather pay the tax than be without their cup of tea.

But the colonists did not share this view. They demanded that the British government remove the tea tax. Dockworkers refused to unload crates of tea from import ships, until they were forced to do so by the governor of Massachusetts, who was loyal to King George.

Bostonians decided it was time to take action. On December 16, 1773, a group of colonists—representatives of the Sons of Liberty—disguised themselves as Native Americans and slipped quietly onto the docks of Boston Harbor. They boarded three ships of the British East India Company and dumped all of the tea into the water. By the end of the night, they had emptied 342 chests of tea, valued at more than 10,000 pounds (almost $19,000). This event became known as the Boston Tea Party.

Parliament responded to the rebels with more laws. British officials passed a series of laws that quickly became known as the "Intolerable Acts." One of the acts ordered Boston Harbor to close until the townspeople paid for the destroyed tea. Another act gave even more power to the governor of Massachusetts. The colonists no longer had any voice in their own government.

"BOSTON NEEDS US"

On July 12, 1774, Dr. William Irvine and a group of other men met at the Presbyterian Church in Carlisle. The room buzzed with excited chatter about all of the events that had been taking place in Boston. Dr. Irvine called the meeting to order. He explained that their brothers in Boston needed their help. It was time to lend support to these colonists in their time of trouble. A hiss of whispers slid through the crowd.

The colonists had trusted King George to be a fair ruler of them. But they now believed that he and Parliament had misused power. They thought it was unfair to make laws for the colonies without the approval or involvement of the colonists. Irvine agreed. He encouraged the men to join their fellow Patriots in a boycott of British goods, to protest the events in Boston. Most of the men gathered there agreed.

That evening, Dr. Irvine and the other men of Carlisle drew up a list of men who would make sure that the townspeople followed the boycott. The name of William Hays appeared on the list.

While the list contained the names of several respected men in Carlisle, it did not contain the name of a single woman. In colonial times, society believed that women should not participate in politics. Women were expected to take care of the children and do domestic chores, such as cooking, cleaning, and mending.

Despite these expectations, many women shared the men's concern about the events in Massachusetts and believed in the principles that were inspiring the boycott. They found their own ways to help.

Mary Hays was one of them. She believed that taxation without representation was wrong, and joined in the boycott of British goods. Because of the boycotts, the colonists in Carlisle had to make their own items. After the dumping of tea in Boston Harbor, women used native plants to make tea. They called them "Liberty Teas." Mary probably brewed teas from red sumac berries, raspberry leaves, spearmint and peppermint leaves, and chamomile.

In Carlisle, Mary and other women gathered together for "spinning bees" to make their own fabric. The fabric they wove was called "homespun." Homespun fabric was rough and scratchy on the skin. It did not look as smooth and polished as Great Britain's fine fabrics. But those who wore homespun clothing were demonstrating their support for those rebelling against British laws. Mary used homespun fabric to sew clothing for herself and William.

The women who supported the Patriots were called the Daughters of Liberty, to show their ties to the Sons of Liberty. Initially formed by a group of young women who vowed to only accept the attention of young men who were willing to fight to the death against the Stamp Act, the Daughters of Liberty grew to include any

Participating in the boycott against British goods, women wove their own homespun fabric to provide a homemade alternative to the finer material imported from England. The process could be time-consuming and tedious, as shown in this reenactment.

woman who believed in the fight for freedom. As the conflict between Great Britain and the colonies dragged on, the Daughters of Liberty would be called on to demonstrate their commitment to their cause.

A CALL TO ARMS

Even after the Boston Massacre, the colonists had different feelings about the British. For many colonists, England was their homeland. About one-fourth of the colonists wanted to stay loyal to the mother country. These colonists were called Loyalists. A third of the colonists wanted to correct what they viewed as injustices enacted by Parliament and King George, and were known as Patriots. The Sons of Liberty were a small group of Patriots who took part in open protests. Still other colonists did not want to take sides in the conflict, choosing to remain neutral. Before long, however, everyone would be forced to make a choice.

On September 5, 1774, Patriot leaders held a convention in Philadelphia. The Patriots wanted to discuss the Intolerable Acts of Parliament. Representatives from all of the colonies except Georgia were present. Georgia had chosen, for the time, to stay loyal to Great Britain. Georgians were fighting their own battle against the Native Americans in the area and desperately needed the support of British soldiers.

Of the 55 delegates to this meeting, Samuel Adams and John Adams represented Massachusetts. From Virginia, George Washington and Patrick Henry served as delegates. The purpose of the meeting was not to push for independence from Britain. Instead, the members wanted to right the wrongs being inflicted

Betsy Ross: Daughter of Liberty

On a warm, sunny afternoon in June 1776, General George Washington and two representatives from the Continental Congress, Robert Morris and George Ross, appeared on the doorstep of a Philadelphia seamstress named Betsy Ross. General Washington knew Betsy well. She had done sewing for him before. Among other things, she had embroidered his shirt ruffles and cuffs. Washington knew that she was skillful at needlework.

According to Ross, Washington pulled out a rough drawing of a flag. Until that time, colonies had used different flags. Washington believed that the Continental Army should be united under one flag. His design included six-pointed stars. Ross pulled out a pair of scissors and showed him how to cut a five-point star in on the colonies. They hoped a unified voice would capture attention in London. The delegates drew up a Declaration of Rights and Grievances, or a statement of complaints, for King George III. The representatives voted to cut off all colonial trade with Great Britain until Parliament lifted the Intolerable Acts. They also approved military training for colonists in case of a war. The town of Carlisle was selected as the location for the

a single snip. The men were impressed with her expert cutting. They immediately hired her to sew the first American flag.

According to legend, this is how the first American flag—with its simple background and cluster of 13 stars, one for each colony—was first created. But today, most historians agree that Betsy Ross was not the person who sewed the first American flag. What is true is that she was a flag maker at the time and probably made many American flags.

Despite the uncertainty about her role in the creation of the first flag, it is known that Betsy Ross was a Daughter of Liberty. She was dedicated to the Patriot cause. She even lost two husbands to the Revolutionary War.

first army arsenal and school. When the session drew to a close in late October, the members agreed to meet again if the situation did not improve. This convention later became known as the First Continental Congress.

Patriot leaders in Massachusetts responded to the approval of military training for colonists by organizing a group of volunteers known as "Minutemen." These Sons of Liberty were prepared to jump into action at all times. They were the first armed soldiers to arrive for battle. They were called Minutemen because they had to be ready to fight "in a minute's notice."

In early April 1775, Patriot leaders received news from London that King George III planned to enforce British rule in the colonies by whatever means were necessary. Leaders sent messengers to towns in eastern Massachusetts, warning the Patriots to be prepared. On April 13, the Massachusetts militia formed six companies of artillery, in preparation for an attack by British troops. They began gathering weapons for battle, storing their supplies in the town of Concord.

Test Your Knowledge

I The French and Indian War was part of a larger conflict. Which one?

   a. The Seven Years War.

   b. The Revolutionary War.

   c. King George's War.

   d. The Frontier Wars.

2 Why did the British Parliament begin passing taxes on the American colonies?

   a. To raise money for exploration of the lands west of the Mississippi River.

   b. To ensure that the colonists did not become too independent.

   c. To pay for the debts from the French and Indian War.

   d. To build a new palace for King George III.

3 How did the Boston Massacre begin?

   a. With the kidnapping of a British customs officer.

   b. With an attack on the militia's supplies of ammunition.

   c. With an acquittal of six British officers accused of murder.

   d. With a snowball fight.

4 What was "Liberty Tea"?

a. Tea dumped in Boston Harbor during
the Boston Tea Party.

b. Tea brewed from native plants to replace
imported tea.

c. Tea sold in containers bearing the seal
of the Sons of Liberty.

d. Illegal tea that was smuggled into the
colonies from the West Indies.

5 What was "homespun" fabric?

a. Fabric that was rough and scratched
the skin.

b. Fabric that was handmade.

c. Fabric used to replace boycotted
British fabrics.

d. All of the above.

ANSWERS: 1. a; 2. c; 3. d; 4. b; 5. d

OUR RIGHTS AND OUR LIBERTIES

A Revolution Begins

As conflict spread through the colonies, Mary Hays went about her daily life. No doubt she heard news of the Continental Congress gathering in Philadelphia. Her husband was charged with enforcing support of the boycott. With workers busy making ammunition at the arsenal in

Carlisle, the tension dividing Loyalist from Patriot probably felt close to home.

On April 16, General Thomas Gage received orders from England commanding him to put down the rebellion by arresting its leaders in Massachusetts. At the time, most leaders in Britain believed that the conflict was largely confined to Massachusetts. If it was stopped there, perhaps no further unrest would trouble the other colonies.

Gage knew that an arrest of key members in the Massachusetts Provincial Congress—like Hancock and Adams—would drain Patriot manpower. But he decided it was more important to snatch up colonial stores at Concord. By seizing the colonists' powder and weapons, he would reduce the risk of a violent rebellion.

Patriot Paul Revere learned of Gage's plans. On the same day, he reported to John Hancock and Samuel Adams in Lexington, on the route from Boston to Concord, warning them that British troops (known as Redcoats for their bright red uniform) were on their way to arrest the two men. Revere then continued on to Concord, where he instructed Patriots there to hide the gunpowder and other weapons stored around the town.

Gage planned to march 600 British soldiers from Boston to Lexington on April 19, 1775. Even though he tried to keep it a secret, news of his plan leaked out. At 10:00 P.M. on the night of April 18, Revere set out on his now famous "midnight ride." All along the road to Lexington, Revere warned townspeople he encountered that British troops were on the move.

Revere finally reached Lexington after midnight. He rode up to the house where Hancock and Adams were staying. The guard outside did not recognize Revere and told him to keep the noise down. "Noise," Revere replied. "You will have noise enough before long. The regulars are coming!"[2] At these words, the guard let him pass, and Revere gave Hancock and Adams his report. They responded by quickly sending a message with the news to the leader of the local militia.

BATTLES IN LEXINGTON AND CONCORD

Patriot Captain John Parker immediately called together a group of about 70 Minutemen. He instructed them to be armed and ready to come running when they heard the drum roll.

At 4:30 A.M. on April 19, a Patriot scout came running up to Captain Parker. He told the captain that the British were less than two miles away. Captain Parker signaled for the drum roll. The Minutemen hurried to Lexington Common in the center of town, ready to fight.

As daylight broke over Lexington, the British Regulars approached the town square. The army of Redcoats had their muskets loaded, expecting to meet 500 colonial soldiers. Instead, they faced a line of about 40 Minutemen. Thirty other men were scattered around the common and in nearby houses.

The British commander, Major Pitcairn, ordered his men to surround and disarm the small militia, but instructed them not to fire. At the same time, Captain Parker ordered his men to disperse. He did not want his small force in a skirmish with fully armed soldiers.

As the Minutemen began to retreat, a single shot rang out. The British soldiers immediately sprang into formation and returned fire. Major Pitcairn screamed at his men to stop shooting.

Finally, the shooting died out. The Regulars marched out of town toward Concord. When the smoke cleared, seven Lexington Minutemen lay dead in the Common. Nine others were wounded. The cries of women and children echoed in the town's streets, and the smell of burnt gunpowder lingered in the air.

Captain Parker shouted for the drum roll. The remaining Minutemen reassembled in the common. The captain calmly told the soldiers that their fellow Patriots in Concord needed their help. The soldiers then set off to face the British again.

In Concord, the Patriots were prepared. As the British neared, 500 Minutemen stopped them at a bridge outside of town. Another battle began. Word quickly spread about the fight. Many men rushed to join their fellow Patriots. Finally, they forced the British to retreat to Boston. Many British soldiers were wounded or killed in the battle.

The random shot in Lexington was later called "the shot heard 'round the world." No one knows for sure who fired that first bullet. But with it, the Revolutionary War began.

UNWELCOME NEWS

News about the battles at Lexington and Concord spread throughout the colonies. One day in April, a messenger on horseback rode into Carlisle. The

townspeople gathered around him to hear the terri-
fying story of Lexington. "A Revolution has begun!"
he exclaimed.

The news of the fighting in Massachusetts must
have shocked Mary Hays. It was clear that the conflict
was growing, and that some felt strongly enough to
vow to fight for freedom. But it was still disturbing
to realize that war was a possibility. The future was
uncertain for Mary and all those living in the colonies.

On May 10, 1775, the Second Continental Congress
met in Philadelphia. Congress delegates elected John
Hancock as their president. At this meeting, they
decided to organize an army. The Congress chose
George Washington to lead their soldiers in the new
military unit, which they named the Continental Army.

In those days, Congress did not have a draft to enlist
soldiers. The military had to rely on volunteers. Throughout the colonies, military recruiters visited towns, trying
to persuade men to join the Continental Army. Most
colonists were farmers, not experienced military men,
but many were eager to fight for their independence.

Because the men were volunteers, many with families and farms or businesses to run, it was difficult to
keep soldiers in the army for long periods of time. The

At the meeting of the Second Continental Congress in 1775, George Washington was chosen as commander-in-chief of the Continental Army.

soldiers agreed to join for one year of service. Minutemen served for only a few months. In July 1775, about 17,000 men had joined the Continental Army. Few remained beyond their year of service. By December, the army had already dwindled to fewer than 6,000 soldiers.

BATTLE OF BUNKER HILL

During the Revolutionary War, the Patriots and the British fought many small battles. Conflict broke out whenever the armies found themselves in close proximity, and many small battles ended as quickly as they had begun. But a few major battles determined the outcome of the war. One of these battles took place at Bunker Hill near Boston.

As the war began, the Continental Army blockaded General Thomas Gage and his British troops in Boston. Washington's troops occupied the hills west of the city. Boston lies on a peninsula jutting north. Further north, across a narrow channel of water, was the Charlestown peninsula. This peninsula was connected to the Massachusetts mainland by an isthmus known as the Charlestown Neck. At the tip of the peninsula was the town of Charlestown. Behind

Charlestown was a hill called Breed's Hill. And behind Breed's Hill rose an even higher peak—Bunker Hill.

General Gage wanted to seize the Charlestown peninsula by going across the harbor to Charlestown. Before he could do this, on the night of June 16, 1775, about 1,500 American troops occupied both hills. They began to build a defense wall on Breed's Hill.

The Patriots worked through the night. As dawn broke, the British were astonished to see the Continental Army blocking their path. They immediately opened fire, and the boom of cannons awakened the sleeping town of Charlestown.

Most of the fighting actually took place on Breed's Hill. General William Howe commanded the British troops at Bunker Hill. Two generals, Artemas Ward and Israel Putnam, led the Patriots. The British soldiers attacked the stronghold, but the Americans drove them back. Again, the Redcoats charged and again they failed, even though the Patriots were running low on ammunition.

Inadequate supplies crippled the British troops. Their attacks on the stronghold should have been followed by artillery fire. But the 6-pound artillery guns had been supplied with 12-pound balls, making them useless.

The British made a final attack. By this time, the Continental Army's ammunition was almost gone. The Redcoats broke through the defense barrier and forced the Patriots to retreat off the peninsula.

At the time, the battle was believed to be a British victory. British troops took over Bunker Hill and secured Boston for nine months. But the Redcoats suffered heavy losses—1,150 men dead or wounded. Of the Patriots, 450 soldiers had been killed or wounded.

The battle was a moral victory for the Patriots. They had made a heroic stand against the British soldiers. They proved to the enemy that they could stand against them. The Battle of Bunker Hill became a rallying cry for the Patriots in battles to come.

INDEPENDENCE DECLARED

Nine months after the Battle at Bunker Hill, the Continental Army had its first major victory at Dorchester Heights near Boston. On March 4, 1776, Patriot troops marched up the hills overlooking Boston Harbor. They began firing cannons at the British troops below. The British retreated out of Boston to their ships and sailed out of the port. The Continental Army had control of Boston.

After this victory, the colonies officially declared their independence from Great Britain. Thomas Jefferson wrote the Declaration of Independence, and the Continental Congress approved it on July 4, 1776. In signing this document, the 13 colonies declared themselves to be free states.

In August 1776, General Howe and his soldiers fought the Patriots in the Battle of Long Island. The American forces were quickly forced to retreat. The British took many Patriots as prisoners. Washington again tried to attack the British and take New York. But he ended up retreating to the Delaware River. It was a dangerous time for the Continental Army. Had Howe captured Washington and his troops, the war would have been over. But Washington escaped.

For several months, the outlook for the Continental Army was grim. They suffered defeat after defeat at the hands of the British. Morale among the troops—and the colonists—was low. A victory was desperately needed.

The Declaration of Independence was drafted by Thomas Jefferson, Benjamin Franklin, John Adams, Robert Livingston, and Roger Sherman, and approved by Congress in July 1776.

On the morning of December 26, 1776, General Washington marched his troops through a snowstorm toward Trenton, New Jersey. From there, the soldiers boarded boats and rowed across the Delaware River. Mercenary soldiers from Germany, known as Hessians, had been hired by the British to guard Trenton. They had spent the night before celebrating the Christmas holiday, and many were still asleep as Washington's troops marched toward them.

Washington and his troops took the Hessian soldiers by surprise in what became known as the Battle of Trenton. After a brief struggle, the Continental Army captured nearly 900 soldiers.

This amazing victory fueled Patriot support. Many more men enlisted in the Continental Army. Once again, the revolution began building momentum. The Americans won another victory at Saratoga, New York in October 1777. There, British General John Burgoyne surrendered his entire army of 5,700 men.

WINTER AT VALLEY FORGE

In 1777, William Hays decided to join the fight for independence. He closed his barbershop and enlisted in the Continental Army. He was accepted, and soon began serving in a unit commanded by Mary's former employer, Dr. Irvine, who was a colonel in Washington's army.

In those days, it was the custom for armies to find a place to camp during the winter months. The British had captured Philadelphia, forcing the Continental Congress to flee, and British troops were wintering in the comfort of the city. Washington needed to find a place for his men. He chose Valley Forge in Pennsylvania.

By this time, the soldiers in the Continental Army were ragged, hungry, and cold. Their uniforms were torn and tattered. Many of them had no shoes or boots. Faced with a snowstorm and icy rains, it took them 8 days to march 13 miles. The feet of those soldiers who had no boots were cracked and bleeding. They tied rags around their bloody feet to keep them from getting worse. Some people said that a person could follow the tracks of the Continental Army by following the blood in the snow. This battered army finally arrived at Valley Forge on December 19, 1777.

The winter months between 1777 and 1778 were bitterly cold at Valley Forge. The poorly clothed soldiers shivered with fevers. Food supplies ran low,

When word of the desperate conditions at Valley Forge spread, many women volunteered to join the camp to care for the soldiers, cooking for them, mending their clothing, and helping to nurse the sick, as shown in this reenactment.

until the troops were forced to forage for something to eat.

Mary Hays soon learned of the suffering of the soldiers at Valley Forge. She was desperate at the thought that her husband might be among those cold and hungry men, and decided to join him at the camp.

Rations without Whiskey

When supplies were plentiful, soldiers received food rations each day and some extra items weekly. As the war dragged on, women began to follow the camp and offer assistance. They often brought their children with them. When women joined the camp, they also received rations. Women were allotted half of a soldier's ration, and children received a quarter of a ration.

What a soldier was given each day varied. Sometimes food was plentiful, and soldiers received a large ration. Other times, food was scarce and rations were smaller. On average, a soldier received 1 pound of beef and 1 pound of fish or 3/4 pound of pork each day. He was given a pound of bread or flour, 1 pint of milk, 1/2 pint of rice, and 1 quart of spruce beer or cider. Each soldier

Mary Hays was quickly put to work at the camp. She cared for the sick and suffering soldiers. She mended their clothes and dressed their wounds. Mary wasn't the only woman at Valley Forge. About 400 women stayed in the camp, helping the army in any way they could. When spring came, Mary decided to stay with Washington's army.

was given three pints of peas, beans, or other vegetables per week. A company of 100 men received 9 gallons of molasses each week. Eventually, a small amount of rum or other alcohol came with the rations. But one regiment stipulated that women and children be given rations without whiskey.

During the winter at Valley Forge, supplies were scarce. Washington sent desperate letters to the Continental Congress, begging for supplies for his cold and starving troops. But the Continental Congress, lacking the ability to tax or collect money, had nothing to give. The men and women encamped in Valley Forge were forced to fend for themselves, gathering whatever scraps of food they could find. Many did not survive the winter.

Test Your Knowledge

I   Which two Patriot leaders did General Gage want to arrest?

     a. Paul Revere and John Adams.

     b. George Washington and Benjamin Franklin.

     c. Samuel Adams and John Hancock.

     d. Thomas Jefferson and Patrick Henry.

2   Where were the first shots fired in the Revolutionary War?

     a. Philadelphia.

     b. Boston.

     c. Yorktown.

     d. Lexington.

3   After which battle did the colonies formally declare their independence?

     a. The Battle at Bunker Hill.

     b. The Battle of Dorchester Heights.

     c. The Battle of Monmouth.

     d. The Battle of Trenton.

4   When William Hays enlisted in the Continental Army, who was the commander of his unit?

     a. Benedict Arnold.

     b. John Paul Jones.

     c. Ethan Allen.

     d. Dr. William Irvine.

5 When Mary Hays joined her husband, where was the Continental Army?

a. Valley Forge, Pennsylvania.

b. Philadelphia, Pennsylvania.

c. Carlisle, Pennsylvania.

d. Germantown, Pennsylvania.

ANSWERS: 1. c; 2. d; 3. b; 4. d; 5. a

Camp Followers

In the struggle for independence, the role of American women was an important—although often neglected—factor in the outcome. Few history books give women the credit they deserve for the contributions they made during the Revolutionary War.

Mary Hays was not the only woman who accompanied the soldiers on their marches. Other women traveled with the army, enduring the same hardships and witnessing the same terrors. These women were called "camp followers." It is difficult to know exactly how many women marched with the Continental Army units. Some records show 800 women with one group—one woman for every 50 men. Other records indicate more than 1,000 women may have accompanied the army.

On the march, Mary Hays and other camp followers performed many of the same duties they did at home. They cooked food, washed and mended clothing, took care of sick and wounded soldiers. Many camp followers carried their children in one arm and pots and pans in the other.

Some women even gave birth to children in the camp. Mary was one of these women. Most women kept their children with them as they marched. If they went into battle with the soldiers, other women cared for their youngsters. The extra noise and commotion of these women and children sometimes annoyed General Washington, especially if they slowed down

Many women were inspired to lend their support to the
cause for independence. Camp followers endured the same
hardships as the soldiers, and often accompanied them
into battle. The reality was far grimmer than this idealized
picture reflects.

the march. But he also understood their importance in the camp.

Many camp followers went with the soldiers onto the battlefield. One British woman accompanied her husband, Sergeant Stone, on the march. She was petite in size, but just as brave as the troops. A soldier wrote, "No consideration of fear could make her leave her husband's side, thro' (through) nine engagements in which he was concerned (fought); in the course of which she twice helped to carry him off wounded from the field of battle."[3] Mrs. Stone ran about the battlefield, bullets whizzing on all sides of her. "At a time when many of our troops were killed," the soldier continued, "she supplied the living with the powder cartridges of the dead."[4] By her actions, many of the men were inspired to fight harder.

Women in the camp also helped keep the soldiers from looking ragged and dirty. In a camp without women, the soldiers did not wash their clothes or bathe. One soldier commented that the men, "not being used to doing things of this sort, choose rather to let their [shirts] rot upon their backs than to be at the trouble of cleaning 'em themselves."[5]

Between battles, the army set up temporary camps. While the men pitched their tents, camp followers gathered firewood. The women cooked a meal with whatever supplies they had. Usually, the soldiers ate meat and dry, flat bread called "hardtack."

Camp women took on all sorts of tasks. Sometimes they butchered cows and other animals for meat. Other times, they tanned goatskin for drumheads. They collected the soldiers' laundry and washed and dried it for them. They took care of many of the more domestic tasks of camp life, so that the soldiers could rest and heal before the next battle.

Despite their valuable service, camp followers were not always appreciated. Women and children who tagged along sometimes slowed the march. At times, General Washington felt that having women around distracted soldiers from the war. When Washington's army marched through Philadelphia in August 1777, he instructed the women to go a different route. "Not a woman belonging to the army is to be seen with the troops on their march through the city," he ordered. "All the rest of the wagons, baggage, and spare horse are to file off to the right," he continued. "Avoid the city entirely, and move onto the bridge at the middle ferry, and there halt."[6]

At the time that Washington gave this order, Mary was with his army. It must have been insulting for Mary, who had cared for the soldiers, to be sent off in another direction, marching with the spare horses.

HARD LIFE IN CAMP

Life for soldiers in the Revolutionary War was a difficult one, and women camp followers shared in the challenges. Food was often stale or spoiled. If the soldiers starved, so did the camp followers. If the soldiers suffered from cold weather, the camp followers suffered with them.

The long marches were hard on the soldiers and followers. After marching all day, they had blisters on their feet. The next day, the blisters would break open and bleed. Several months of travel would wear out their boots. In the field, soldiers could not always find shoes. They walked barefoot or tied scraps of cloth around their feet.

The women and children in the camp were exposed to all the same hazards of war as the men. As they

On the Home Front

Many colonial women helped the Continental Army without ever seeing a battle. Women at home also played an important role in the fight for independence. Throughout the colonies, women donated their pewter dishes to be made into musket balls. They spun and wove cloth for uniforms and blankets. Many women carried supplies over miles of rough land to bring them to the soldiers.

At home, women took over the chores and work normally performed by their husbands. Women ran shops and businesses. They did all the farm work—ploughed, planted, weeded, and harvested. They made grain into bread. In New York and Philadelphia, women visited Patriot prisoners in the British jails. Whenever a battle took place near a town, the women rushed out to nurse the sick and wounded soldiers. They brought bandages and hospital supplies.

It was this critical support from women, both on and off the field, which contributed to an American victory. During the Revolutionary War, women took on tasks they never would have otherwise attempted, and discovered new strengths and skills that would, for a time, transform their lives.

walked along with the baggage train, they risked being ambushed, captured, or even killed.

Disease became a big problem in army camps. Smallpox and measles spread from soldier to soldier. Many Patriots suffered upset stomachs from spoiled food, unsanitary living conditions, or bad water. During the Revolutionary War, medical treatment and medicines were scarce. More soldiers died from disease than in battles.

Test Your Knowledge

1 What was the term for women and children who accompanied the Continental Army?

    a. Aides-de-camp.

    b. Camp followers.

    c. Camp families.

    d. The family brigade.

2 What tasks did women who accompanied the Continental Army perform?

    a. Mended clothes.

    b. Cooked food.

    c. Nursed the sick.

    d. All of the above.

3 What was "hardtack"?

    a. A stiff, flat bread.

    b. Dry meat cooked over a campfire.

    c. Tanned goatskin used for drumheads.

    d. A type of saddle.

4 How did General Washington view the women who accompanied the army?

    a. As a vital component of the fight against the British.

    b. As a welcome addition to camp life.

    c. As a noisy distraction.

    d. As potential spies.

5 What dangers did women face in the army camp?

a. Disease.

b. Starvation.

c. Freezing temperatures.

d. All of the above.

ANSWERS: 1. b; 2. d; 3. a; 4. c; 5. d

Other Battlefield Heroines

W hile Mary Hays (as "Molly Pitcher") has become
a celebrated heroine of the Revolutionary War,
there were other women who demonstrated courage
and heroism during the fight for independence. These
women either fought on the field or served as spies
for the Patriot armies. One of these heroines was a

16-year-old girl from South Carolina named Dicey Langston.

Just like her brothers, Dicey was a full-blooded Patriot. She was a strong and independent girl, who could ride a horse and handle a rifle as expertly as anyone she knew. When the war began, Dicey's brothers ran off to join the Continental Army. Her father, Solomon, was too old to fight as a soldier. He and Dicey stayed home on their plantation.

Being a Patriot in the South was dangerous. Many Southerners were Loyalists. Dicey and her father risked being attacked by British supporters.

Each Sunday, the Langstons got together with their relatives for dinner. Dicey and her father were the only Patriots. Even though members of the family were political enemies, they tried to enjoy their weekly meal together. But at the table, the biggest topic of conversation was the war. During dinner, Dicey listened closely to everything her relatives said. They often talked about Loyalist plans. After they had finished eating, Dicey would run off to her brothers' camp and tell them everything she had heard.

At first, Dicey's relatives spoke freely in front of her. They thought that she was just a child and didn't understand their conversation. However, they soon became suspicious when their plans always seemed to leak to the Patriots.

Loyalists warned Solomon to keep his daughter quiet. Afraid he would lose his plantation or be hurt, Solomon begged Dicey to stop carrying messages to her brothers. Dicey wanted to protect her father, so she agreed.

However, her silence lasted only a few weeks. One of the Loyalist groups working in the area was called the Bloody Scouts. They had been given the name because of the cruel and ruthless attacks they made on defenseless plantations. Dicey overheard that the Bloody Scouts were going to raid a small Patriot settlement called Little Eden. This village was near her brothers' camp.

Dicey knew that the people at Little Eden would be taken completely by surprise. No doubt, some of them would be killed. Even more frightening, the Bloody Scouts might discover her brothers' camp and murder them as well. She had to get word to her brothers about the attack.

The young Patriot did not want her father to know of her plans. Dicey had promised him that she would not go to the Patriot camp. Also, if she told Solomon about

Women often disguised themselves as men to serve as soldiers or spies during the war. In this illustration, women intelligence riders from South Carolina are shown intercepting British dispatches, which they then carried to the Continental Army commander camped nearby.

her plans, he might be blamed if she was discovered. Loyalists would use it as an excuse to kill him and take his property.

That night, when everyone was asleep, Dicey crept quietly out of the house. She ran through woods and fields, trying to stay hidden from sight. She made good progress until she came to a flooded creek. Dicey wasn't sure how deep the water was, but knowing that it was urgent that her message reach the Continental Army, she waded into the water.

The current was quicker than she had thought. Suddenly, she lost her footing and got carried away in the swirling water. She fought her way back to shore. But when she climbed out of the creek, she had no idea where she was. She decided to trust her instincts. Luckily, she was right.

After hours of walking, Dicey finally made it to the camp. Breathlessly, she told her brothers about the planned attack on Little Eden. The soldiers set out to warn the helpless settlement.

When the Bloody Scouts arrived at Little Eden the next morning, they found it abandoned. The gang boiled with rage. Meanwhile, Dicey was back at the plantation, dressed, and eating breakfast with her family. She had made a 20-mile trip overnight. Her father never suspected her nighttime adventure.

The Bloody Scouts returned to the area, determined to have revenge for their thwarted attack.

They immediately suspected Solomon and Dicey. The gang arrived at Solomon's plantation, ready to kill him. One of the men pointed his pistol at Solomon's head and cocked it. Immediately, Dicey jumped in front of the gun and scolded the Scout for threatening to kill an old man. Another gang member told the man to lower his gun, and the two men got into an argument. In the heat of the new fight, the gang members forgot their original mission. They left the plantation furious with each other. Dicey had saved the lives of her father and the people at Eden Hill.

FLOUR FOR A SPY

During the Revolution, British troops often seized private homes for the use of their army. They transformed them into offices, meeting places, or mess halls. British forces occupied Philadelphia in September 1777. Lydia Darragh's home was a block away from the wharves and across the street from General Howe's headquarters. Howe chose to use one of Lydia's rooms for his officers. This decision ultimately led to his undoing. Lydia's house brought about Howe's defeat in what would have otherwise been a victory over Washington's army.

When it came to the struggle for independence, Lydia Darragh was quite outspoken, open in her criticism of British actions and in her support for the Patriots. She even violated her religion as a Quaker. Quakers do not believe in violence or in war. But Lydia became what was known as a "Fighting Quaker"—one of a group who kept their faith even while they took part in the war. She did everything she could to help Washington's forces.

A Tasty Message

Emily Geiger was another woman who played a valuable role during the Revolutionary War. She served the Continental Army as a messenger. She lived near General Greene's camp, by the Broad River in South Carolina. Greene wanted someone to carry a message to General Sumter, who was then camped on the Wateree. In the letter, Greene asked Sumter's men to join him for an attack on the British.

In order to get the message to Sumter, the messenger would have to travel through miles of Loyalist territory. It was difficult to find a man willing to take on such a dangerous mission. Finally, 18-year-old Emily Geiger volunteered. Greene was impressed by the young woman's bravery.

On the way, Emily was stopped by Loyalists. The scouts noticed that Emily had come from the direction

On December 2, 1777, one of Howe's officers came to Lydia. He told her that they would be using one of her rooms for a meeting at seven o'clock that evening. He also requested that her family go to bed early so that the British could have their privacy.

The confidential manner of the meeting made Lydia curious. That night, she pretended to be asleep. But when the meeting started, she slipped out of bed and

of Greene's camp. When they questioned her, Emily tried to lie. However, the young Patriot was not a very good liar and blushed with her answers. The men took her to Fort Granby to be questioned by a British officer.

Hesitating to touch the young woman, the scouts decided not to search her. They locked her in a room to wait for an officer. Emily pulled out her letter and ate it, piece by piece. When the British officer arrived, he searched her, but found nothing. Satisfied, he released her.

Emily continued on her way to General Sumter. When she arrived, she told him her story and recited the message from memory. Emily's quick thinking ensured that a unified force attacked the British, resulting in an important victory.

crept up to the door. Lydia bent down, put her ear to the keyhole, and listened.

She heard a British officer reading an order for the troops. "On the night of the fourth," he said, "we will march out of the city and attack Washington's men at Whitemarsh (a town north of Philadelphia)."[7]

When the officers were getting ready to leave, she hurried back to her bedroom. The British officers came to her room to ask her to let them out. Lydia waited for them to knock three times before she opened the door. She wanted them to think that she had been asleep.

However, after the officers left, Lydia was anything but tired. She knew she must somehow get the information to Washington. Lydia also knew that if the British found her to be a spy, she would be hanged.

The next day, Lydia told her husband that she had to go outside the city to Frankford for flour. She walked across the street to General Howe. "I would like to pass through the lines to go to the flour mill," she announced.[8] Suspecting nothing, Howe agreed to let her pass. With a flour sack flung over her shoulder, Lydia set out to find the Continental Army.

Lydia did actually stop at the flour mill. But she left her bag there and continued on her way. As she walked toward Washington's line, she ran into one of his patrols. Luckily, she knew one of the men. It was not safe for her to reveal to the whole patrol that she was a spy. So she asked to speak with her friend in private.

"You must promise not to reveal me as the source of this information," Lydia pleaded.[9] Her friend agreed to keep her identity secret. She then told him about General Howe's plan. The soldier thanked her for the news and galloped off to deliver the message to Washington.

Lydia returned to the mill, picked up her flour, and walked back to Philadelphia. For the next few days, Lydia worried that her role as an informant might be discovered. On the night of December 4, the British marched out as planned, still thinking that they would take Washington by surprise.

However, Washington was prepared for the attack. Howe and his men returned to Philadelphia in defeat. The next evening, a British officer grabbed Lydia by the arm, dragged her into a room, and locked the door. He questioned her about her family.

"Had anyone not been in bed the night of the meeting?" he demanded. "Could anyone have listened at the door?"[10] He asked question after question.

Lydia stayed perfectly calm, assuring the British officer that the family had been asleep by eight o'clock. The officer did not ask Lydia about her own whereabouts on the night of the meeting. He was sure that she had been asleep, because it took her so long to answer her door. Lydia's plan had worked, and she saved the Continental Army from a devastating defeat.

MARY SLOCUMB'S NIGHTMARE

When the fight for independence began in North Carolina, Mary Slocumb was 16 years old. She was the beautiful new bride of Ezekiel Slocumb, known as Zeke.

In May 1775, a group of Patriots met in Charlotte, North Carolina, and elected to reject the rule of King George III and pledged their loyalty to the Continental Congress. Zeke Slocumb attended the meeting and became a Patriot.

However, the governor of North Carolina was a Loyalist. He called for all loyal British colonists to come together at Wilmington. He planned to form a militia to fight the Patriots.

The Patriots wanted to cut off the Loyalists before they reached Wilmington. From Charlotte, they marched toward Moore's Creek Bridge, about

18 miles from Wilmington. This bridge was an important target. The Loyalists would have to cross it in order to get to town.

On the night of February 26, the Patriots reached the bridge and set up their trap. They pulled up the floorboards of the bridge to make crossing it nearly impossible. The Patriots then smeared the remaining beams with animal fat and soap to make them slippery. After they were finished, they hid behind nearby bushes and waited for the enemy.

Meanwhile, Mary Slocumb was at home, asleep in her bed. She had a terrible nightmare. In her dream, she saw a battlefield covered with dead and dying soldiers. She wandered the field until she came to a man wrapped in a cloak. She recognized the coat as her husband's. At that moment, Mary awoke with a scream.

Terrified, Mary paced her room, wondering what to do. The dream was too real to be ignored. She dressed in her riding clothes and called in her servant. "I must go to Zeke," she announced.[11]

Mary Slocumb rushed to the stables and saddled her fastest mare. She galloped down the road in the direction of Moore's Creek. Along the way, she

Deborah Samson was another heroine of the Revolutionary War, who disguised herself as a man to join the fight for independence.

replayed the nightmare in her mind. She was certain she would find her husband dead.

She rode through the night. Early the next morning, Mary heard what she believed to be a roll of thunder. She pulled her horse to a halt. She listened carefully. Another rumble echoed in the distance, a rumble that sounded like the noise of cannons being fired. She rode on, faster than before.

Before long, she found herself in the middle of the battle. The sounds of muskets and rifles echoed all around her. Suddenly, she was surrounded by the images of her nightmare. Under a cluster of trees, she saw wounded and dying men. As she scanned the area, she saw something that made her jump down from her horse. On the ground, a body was wrapped in her husband's cloak. Mary's nightmare had come true.

She rushed to the body and flung open the wrap. She saw "a face clothed with gore from a dreadful wound across the temple." [12] The man was so covered in blood that Mary could not tell who it was. She touched the man's face. He was still warm. He begged for water. But Mary did not recognize his voice.

Mary quickly searched for a kettle. She ran to the stream and filled it with water. She poured some in the man's mouth and rinsed his face. The man was not her husband, but a friend, Frank Codgell. Slowly, he began to regain his senses.

"Mary," he moaned. "My head is not what is killing me. It is the pain in my leg." [13]

Mary looked down and saw a puddle of blood at his feet. She grabbed a knife and cut open his pant leg. There, she could see that a bullet had shot through his calf. Mary did not have any bandages for the wound. But she found some leaves to fill the hole and stop the bleeding.

There were about 20 other men scattered on the ground around her that were also hit. After she made sure that Codgell was comfortable, she ran from soldier to soldier nursing each one. While she was working, her husband found her. He was "as bloody as a butcher and muddy as a ditcher," but he was all right.[14]

Mary stayed at the battlefield all day and late into the night. The Patriots won a tremendous victory over the Loyalists. Thanks to Mary's nursing, only one Patriot died that day.

MARGARET CORBIN, CANNON GIRL

The story of Margaret Corbin has much in common with the story of Mary Hays. When the war began, Margaret's husband John enlisted in the Continental Army. She joined the army as a camp follower, and soldiers also called her "Molly Pitcher."

On November 16, 1776, British forces attacked Fort Washington, New York, where Margaret and John were stationed. The army of 2,800 Patriots fought to hold the fort against nearly 9,000 British troops. During the battle, Margaret's husband was killed at his cannon. There was no one else to fire it. So Margaret ran to the cannon and began to load and fire it herself. She continued firing until she was hit by a bullet and fell to the ground, seriously wounded.

The forces were too unevenly matched for any hope of a victory for the Continental troops. Before long, the British forces captured Fort Washington. They took most of the survivors as prisoners. Somehow, Margaret managed to escape. But her arm was almost completely blown off, leaving her badly handicapped. In those days, it was difficult for a woman to survive on her own, especially if she needed constant care.

In 1779, the state of Pennsylvania recognized Margaret Corbin's heroism. State officials awarded her 30 dollars of relief money. The Continental Congress also gave her a soldier's pension at half the rate and an annual outfit of clothing. Margaret Corbin was the first woman in the United States to get a pension. In honor of her heroism, she became known to many as "Captain Molly."

Test Your Knowledge

1 How did Dicey Langston aid the Continental Army?

    a. By providing them with details of Loyalist plans.

    b. By spying on British officers as they outlined their battle strategies.

    c. By providing food and water to the soldiers.

    d. By carrying messages between George Washington and his officers.

2 Who were the "Bloody Scouts"?

    a. A division of the British Army known for its fierce fighting.

    b. A violent gang of Loyalists.

    c. A group of spies traveling through the south to extract information from plantation owners.

    d. A unit of the Continental Army under the command of Benedict Arnold.

3 What information did Lydia Darragh carry to Washington's army?

    a. That their supplies had been ambushed at Whitemarsh.

    b. That a French fleet was sailing toward Virginia.

    c. That British troops were occupying Philadelphia.

    d. That the British were planning an attack on December 4.

4 What was Mary Slocumb's nightmare?

   a. That British troops would burn her
      family's farm.

   b. That she would find her husband's body
      in a field of dead and dying soldiers.

   c. That her husband and his close friend would
      be shot and killed in battle.

   d. That she would find herself caring for hundreds
      of wounded men.

5 What was Margaret Corbin called by the soldiers
in her husband's unit?

   a. Captain Cannon.

   b. Brave Maggie.

   c. Molly Pitcher.

   d. Emily Geiger.

ANSWERS: 1. a; 2. b; 3. d; 4. b; 5. c

Sergeant
Molly

In June 1777, British General John Burgoyne and 6,000 Regulars pushed down from Canada into upstate New York. Meanwhile, the Continental Army enjoyed victories at Germantown and Brandywine Creek. On July 6, the British recaptured Fort Ticonderoga in New York without a struggle. They had another victory at Oriskany. As

Burgoyne marched south, the Patriots destroyed bridges, chopped down trees in the British path, and fired at the Redcoats from the surrounding woods. They hoped to slow the British march. Eventually, the British soldiers began running low on supplies.

Burgoyne moved slowly through the wilderness along the Hudson River. His dragging speed allowed the Americans time to build a fort in a wooded area about 40 miles north of Albany, at Saratoga. On September 19, Burgoyne attacked the fort. The British met American forces in a clearing on a nearby farm. This place became known as Freeman's Farm. Nightfall saved the British from utter defeat.

On October 7, Burgoyne led a second attack. American forces—led by General Benedict Arnold—won the second fight at Freeman's Farm. The victory at the Battle of Saratoga was a huge leap for the Patriots. The Americans took 6,000 prisoners and large amounts of supplies. About 600 British soldiers were killed or wounded. Only about 150 Patriots were killed in battle. The American victory destroyed all British hopes of dividing the colonies along the Hudson River.

After the Battle of Saratoga, France believed that the Patriots might be able to win the war. In February 1778,

France agreed to help the Americans fight the British. The French hoped to win back some land they had lost to the British during the French and Indian War. Later, Spain and Holland also supported the Patriots in their struggle against Great Britain.

In the spring, the British forces received word that the French fleet was on its way to America. British leader Sir Henry Clinton worried that if his army stayed in Philadelphia, it would be surrounded by hostile forces. He believed that the French would soon control the Chesapeake Bay and the Delaware River. In so doing, the American forces would drive a wedge between the British in New York and Pennsylvania. On June 18, 1778, Clinton began to move his army toward the safe haven of New York City.

General Washington and his troops set off after Clinton's army. William and Mary Hays were with the soldiers. On June 28, the Continental Army caught up with the British near Monmouth, New Jersey. General Charles Lee led a brief skirmish with the Redcoats. He learned that British reinforcements were on their way. Lee panicked and ordered the Continental forces to retreat.

As they retreated, the soldiers met General Washington. Astonished, Washington ordered them to turn back around and continue fighting. The soldiers managed to reorganize their lines, and soon were again engaged in combat.

CARRYING WATER

During the Battle of Monmouth, Mary Hays was busy on the field. Soldiers operating cannons needed a constant supply of water. In order to work properly, the cannon barrel had to be cleaned after each fire. The soldiers used a long rod with a wet rag tied at the end of it—called a rammer—to clean out the barrels. The cloth removed sparks and gunpowder from the inside of the cannon. Camp followers, like Mary, ran about the battlefield, wetting down the swabbing rods.

That blistering June 28 was almost unbearably hot. Temperatures reached a scorching 100 degrees. Soldiers on both sides were exhausted by the heat. One by one, they dropped to the ground, their throats parched. Some men became so dehydrated that their tongues swelled and they couldn't speak.

That day, Mary Hays not only brought water to the cannon soldiers. She ran to soldiers who had collapsed

Mary Hays assisted her husband during the Battle of Monmouth, bringing him water and jumping in to swab and load his cannon when he was shot.

on the field with a pitcher of water for them to drink. The smell of burnt gunpowder stung her nostrils. She was covered in filth and grime. Her clothes were soaked with blood and sweat. Artillery fire whistled at every turn. But Mary pushed on. She knew that the soldiers needed her.

Many of the soldiers did not know her name. They called her "Molly." Through the thick smoke and deafening gunfire, she heard voices call, "Molly, bring me the pitcher!" Others, short of breath, simply yelled, "Molly! Pitcher!"

The name stuck. Years later, a woman who lived across the street from Mary Hays in Carlisle said, "I heard her say she carried water to the men on the battlefield. . . . She was known pretty commonly as Mollie Pitcher; that was what we called her."[15]

Throughout the battle, Mary cared for her husband, as well as the other soldiers. She brought him water and stood beside him several times. By watching him, she learned how to load and fire a cannon. When William was suddenly struck by gunfire and fell to the ground unconscious, Mary knew what to do. She took over her husband's cannon, grabbed the rammer, and began to "swab and load."

The battle stretched on for 12 hours, making it the longest battle of the American Revolution. During the night, the British silently retreated. As dawn broke the next morning, the Americans saw that the Redcoats had abandoned their position. The Continental forces had won the Battle of Monmouth. It was a triumph for Washington's army, and for Mary Hays.

The day after the Battle of Monmouth, General Washington ordered his soldiers to assemble. He called

For her heroism during the Battle of Monmouth, Hays was made a noncommissioned officer of the Continental Army by General Washington.

for Mary Hays to come before him. She walked up to Washington and saluted him.

Because of her heroic deeds on the battlefield, Washington made Mary a noncommissioned officer of the Continental Army. From that day forward, she was to be known as Sergeant Molly. The soldiers clapped and cheered.

Mary Hays, now known as Molly Pitcher, nursed her wounded husband back to health. She continued to march with the army, nursing the sick and wounded and carrying pitchers of water onto the battlefield.

In 1780, Molly gave birth to a son, who was named John. Even as a new mother, Molly remained with the Continental Army.

INDEPENDENCE!

After 1779, much of the fighting moved to the southern colonies. In the south, British forces won many of the battles. They quickly took control of Georgia. In 1780, British soldiers also captured Charleston, South Carolina. During the attack, Redcoats took more than 5,000 colonists as prisoners.

In March 1781, American troops met the British near Greensboro, North Carolina. They fought the Battle of Guilford Courthouse. There, Patriots forced the enemy to retreat. After several small battles, American troops pushed the British completely out of North Carolina. The British retreated to Charleston, South Carolina, and Savannah, Georgia. After these battles, the Continental Army controlled large portions of the southern territory.

Not all colonists supported the Continental Army. Almost 80,000 people left the colonies after the

Declaration of Independence was signed. Many southerners who were Loyalists remained to fight the Patriots. In October 1780, the Loyalists fought the Patriots at the Battle of King's Mountain in South Carolina. The Patriots won an overwhelming

General George Washington

Imagine what it would be like to meet one of your heroes—a celebrity, an athlete, or some other famous person. What would it be like if he or she complimented you, praising you for some job you had done? That is probably the way Molly Pitcher felt when General Washington congratulated her on her bravery in the Battle of Monmouth. Nearly every soldier in the Continental Army looked up to Washington. Many of those soldiers never received any special attention from the general. At a time when women went virtually unnoticed, Molly Pitcher was publicly praised by one of the most popular men in the fight for independence.

George Washington was born in 1732 to a Virginia planter. In 1754, he was commissioned as a lieutenant colonel in the colonial militia and fought in the first skirmishes that led to the French and Indian War. During that war, he served as an aide to a British victory, killing 150 Loyalists and capturing 600 others. This win helped bring an end to Loyalist support in the former colonies. British supporters were afraid to openly admit their loyalty to the king, and many fled America.

general, Edward Braddock. Washington escaped any injury, even though four bullets ripped his coat and two horses were shot and killed from beneath him.

From 1759 until the start of the American Revolution, Washington managed his lands around Mount Vernon and served in the Virginia House of Burgesses. At the Second Continental Congress in May 1775, delegates elected Washington to be the commander-in-chief of the Continental Army. He took command of the soldiers on July 3, 1775, at Cambridge, Massachusetts.

Washington took his army of inexperienced, poorly equipped men and turned them into soldiers who could beat the highly trained British Regulars. He proved to be an excellent commander and gained the respect of his men. After the war, Washington became the first president of the United States in 1789.

The final battle of the war began in September 1781 at Yorktown, Virginia. There, General Cornwallis and an army of 7,000 British soldiers waited for a supply ship. General Washington learned that a French fleet was on its way to North America. He decided to combine French and Patriot forces in an attack on Yorktown.

The American forces trapped the British Army. The French fleet barricaded the Chesapeake Bay port so that no supplies could arrive by sea. On land, the Continental Army and French troops kept the British from retreating out of the town. On October 17, 1781, Cornwallis surrendered. The fighting was not completely ended, but the battle at Yorktown marked the true end of major combat in the Revolutionary War.

On September 3, 1783, American and British leaders signed the Treaty of Paris, bringing an end to the Revolutionary War. The 13 former colonies had gained their independence. They named their new country the United States of America. In September 1788, the U.S. government approved a new constitution for the new nation. George Washington became the first president of the United States in 1789.

MOLLY'S SPIRIT OF FREEDOM

After the war ended in 1783, William and Molly returned to Carlisle. William reopened his barbershop and tried to resume his life as it had been before the war. Molly was busy tending to household chores and caring for her young son, John.

In 1785, the Hays family had a visitor—an army veteran named Pearce Rannals. Rannals had no place to live, so William and Molly graciously invited him into their home. However, Rannals soon caused trouble for the couple. When he shopped at local stores, he told the clerks that he was William's brother. Rannals charged his expenses to William's account. Soon, he pushed William and Molly deep into debt. One night, Rannals left town, taking with him William's musket, gunpowder, and a pair of his fancy shoe buckles.

In 1786, William Hays died, leaving his wife to deal with their large debt. Molly Pitcher tried to save the family home but was forced to sell half of her land in order to pay her debtors.

In 1793, Molly married another war veteran—John McCauley. McCauley had been a friend of William Hays and had fought with him in the war. Like his new wife, McCauley could not write—both of them signed their marriage papers with an "X" instead of their names.

McCauley worked hauling rocks and clay for the Carlisle prison. Unfortunately, John McCauley and Molly Pitcher suffered an unhappy marriage. Apparently, McCauley had a violent temper. In 1794, Molly's neighbor, Jane Anderson, accused McCauley of attacking her, and McCauley admitted that she was correct. At some point between 1807 and 1810, John McCauley suddenly disappeared. No one knows for certain what ever happened to him.

Molly Pitcher continued to live in Carlisle. She was hired by the town to clean, wash, and paint some buildings around town. She took whatever work was necessary to help support herself and her son. Her hard life made her a tough woman, but her inner compassion always seemed to shine through. She often helped nurse the sick. "She was so rough and coarse," one person who knew her remembered. "[But] the roughness was on the outside . . . she would always visit the sick and was always willing to sit up at night with the sick." [16]

In 1822, the state government of Pennsylvania finally awarded Molly an annual payment of 40 dollars

Molly Pitcher has become a symbol of women who performed heroically during the Revolutionary War. Today she is honored with a memorial at the site of the Monmouth Battlefield, where the Battle of Monmouth is reenacted annually.

for her bravery during the war. As Molly grew older, she became nearly blind in one eye. Even still, one friend said she was "healthy, active and strong, fleshy and short, [and] passionately fond of children."[17] The people of Carlisle would often see her walking down the streets, wearing a striped skirt, wool stockings, ankle-high boots, and a ruffled cap over her tousled gray hair.

Long after her heroic acts during the Revolutionary War, Molly Pitcher's contribution was honored by these women of the Molly Pitcher Brigade, who are shown shooting at a police rifle range in Spring Lake in the 1940s.

On January 22, 1832, Molly Pitcher died. At the time of her death, she was thought to be 78 years old. She lived a humble life, but was remembered by her friends for her bravery during the war. A Carlisle newspaper praised her courage and valor, stating that she had "lived during the days of the American Revolution, shared its hardships, and witnessed many a scene of blood."[18] In recognition of her contribution during the war, Molly was buried with military honors.

It took many years before Molly was not only recognized, but also celebrated as a Revolutionary War heroine. Today, people honor the contribution Molly Pitcher made to America's independence. In Carlisle, a monument and cannon pay tribute to her life. In Freehold, New Jersey, at the Monmouth battlefield site, a memorial heralds her bravery. Even a highway bears her name—Molly Pitcher Highway leads travelers into Carlisle, Pennsylvania. She reminds all Americans of the contributions many women made during the Revolutionary War, in service to the spirit of freedom.

Test Your Knowledge

I Soldiers called for water on the battlefield when they were thirsty. Why else did they need water during a battle?

   a. To wipe clean their bayonets.

   b. To make gunpowder.

   c. To moisten their rifles.

   d. To clean their cannons.

2 Why did Molly Pitcher begin firing the cannon in the Battle of Monmouth?

   a. She wanted revenge on the British soldiers who had murdered her husband.

   b. She took over for her husband when he was shot.

   c. Washington ordered her to begin firing when many of his men collapsed from exhaustion.

   d. She wanted to help and could not carry any more water.

3 What honor did Washington give to Molly Pitcher?

   a. He made her a noncommissioned officer in the Continental Army.

   b. He appointed her to serve as his official aide.

   c. He made her a commander of a small unit of female volunteers.

   d. He appointed her to organize and direct the activities of all camp followers.

4 Who was John McCauley?

   a. A veteran who briefly lived with Mary and William Hays before robbing them and leaving them to repay his debts.

   b. The Continental Army officer responsible for the victory at Yorktown.

   c. Molly Pitcher's second husband.

   d. The governor of Pennsylvania who awarded Molly Pitcher an annual payment for her service in the war.

5 What work did Molly Pitcher perform after her husband abandoned her?

   a. She was a nurse.

   b. She was a seamstress.

   c. She washed, cleaned, and painted buildings.

   d. She was a teacher.

ANSWERS: 1. d; 2. b; 3. a; 4. c; 5. c

1754 The year it is believed that Mary Ludwig was born in New Jersey.

1765 Parliament passes the Stamp Act; violent protests begin in Boston.

1766 Great Britain ends the Stamp Act.

1767 Parliament passes the Townshend Acts, which tax glass, lead, paint, paper and tea.

1768 Mary Ludwig leaves her farm home to work for the Irvines in Carlisle, Pennsylvania.

1769 Mary Ludwig marries William Hays on July 24.

1770 Five colonists die in the Boston Massacre on March 5.

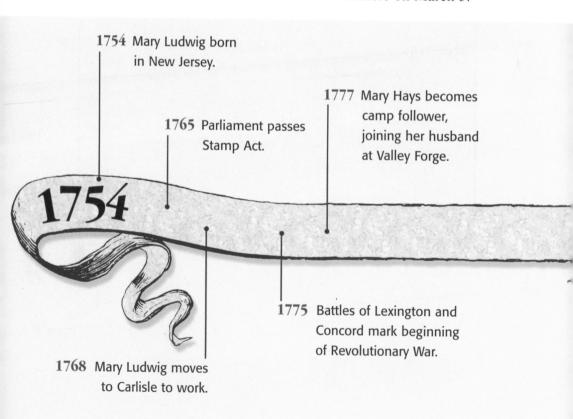

1754 Mary Ludwig born in New Jersey.

1765 Parliament passes Stamp Act.

1777 Mary Hays becomes camp follower, joining her husband at Valley Forge.

1768 Mary Ludwig moves to Carlisle to work.

1775 Battles of Lexington and Concord mark beginning of Revolutionary War.

1773   Colonists dump 342 chests of tea into Boston Harbor on December 13; this event becomes known as the Boston Tea Party.

1774   Parliament responds to the Boston Tea Party by passing the Intolerable Acts and closing Boston Harbor; the First Continental Congress is held on September 5.

1775   Battles of Lexington and Concord are fought on April 19, beginning the Revolutionary War; the Second Continental Congress is held; George Washington elected commander-in-chief of the Continental Army.

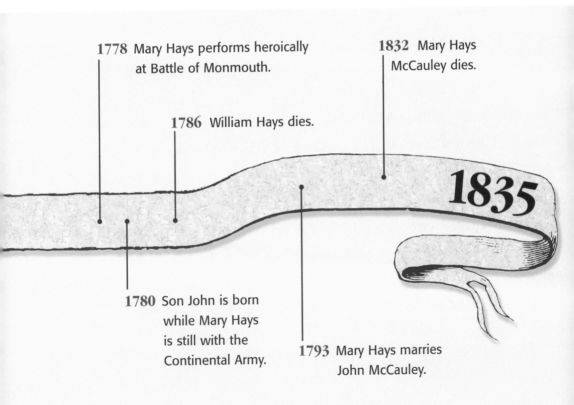

1778 Mary Hays performs heroically at Battle of Monmouth.

1832 Mary Hays McCauley dies.

1786 William Hays dies.

1835

1780 Son John is born while Mary Hays is still with the Continental Army.

1793 Mary Hays marries John McCauley.

1776   Patriots win their first major battle at Dorchester Heights, near Boston, on March 4; the Declaration of Independence is signed on July 4; Washington leads a surprise attack on British forces in the Battle of Trenton on December 26.

1777   William Hays joins the Continental Army; Mary becomes a camp follower; American soldiers spend a harsh winter at Valley Forge.

1778   Mary takes over William's cannon at the Battle of Monmouth on June 28, becomes Sergeant Molly; France agrees to join the American forces.

1780   Mary and William Hays have a son, John.

1781   The British surrender at Yorktown on October 17.

1783   Mary and William Hays return to Carlisle; Treaty of Paris is signed on September 3, officially ending the war.

1786   William Hays dies.

1789   George Washington becomes the first president of the United States.

1793   Mary Hays marries John McCauley.

1807–1810   During this period, John McCauley disappears.

1822   Mary Hays McCauley is awarded 40 dollars per year by the state of Pennsylvania.

1832   Mary Hays McCauley ("Molly Pitcher") dies in Carlisle on January 22.

CHAPTER 2
Working Girl

1 Eileen Dunn Bertanzetti, *Molly Pitcher* (Philadelphia: Chelsea House Publishers, 2002), 16.

CHAPTER 4
A Revolution Begins

2 David Hackett Fischer, *Paul Revere's Ride* (New York: Oxford University Press, 1994), 109.

CHAPTER 5
Camp Followers

3 Holly A. Mayer, *Belonging to the Army: Camp Followers and Community During the American Revolution* (Columbia, S.C.: University of South Carolina Press, 1996), 9.

4 Ibid.

5 Walter Hart Blumenthal, *Women Camp Followers of the American Revolution* (New York: Arno Press, 1974), 62.

6 Ibid., 65.

CHAPTER 6
Other Battlefield Heroines

7 Paul Engle, *Women in the American Revolution* (Chicago: Follett Publishing Company, 1976), 12.

8 Ibid.

9 Ibid., 13.

10 Ibid., 15.

11 Ibid., 19.

12 Ibid., 20.

13 Ibid.

14 Ibid., 21.

CHAPTER 7
Sergeant Molly

15 Bertanzetti, 60.

16 Ibid., 69.

17 Ibid., 69–70.

18 Ibid., 70.

Bibliography

Bertanzetti, Eileen Dunn. *Molly Pitcher*. Philadelphia: Chelsea House Publishers, 2002.

Blumenthal, Walter Hart. *Women Camp Followers of the American Revolution*. New York: Arno Press, 1974.

Claghorn, Charles. *Women Patriots of the American Revolution*. Metuchen, N.J.: Scarecrow Press, 1991.

Engle, Paul. *Women in the American Revolution*. Chicago: Follett Publishing Company, 1976.

Fischer, David Hackett. *Paul Revere's Ride*. New York: Oxford University Press, 1994.

Mayer, Holly A. *Belonging to the Army: Camp Followers and Community During the American Revolution*. Columbia, S.C.: University of South Carolina Press, 1996.

Norton, Mary Beth. *Liberty's Daughters: The Revolutionary Experience of American Women: 1750–1800*. Boston: Little Brown, 1980.

Roberts, Cokie. *Founding Mothers: The Women Who Raised Our Nation*. New York: William Morrow, 2004.

Young, Philip. *Revolutionary Ladies*. New York: Knopf, 1977.

WEBSITES

www.rootsweb.com/~pacumber/molly.htm

Bertanzetti, Eileen Dunn. *Molly Pitcher*. Philadelphia: Chelsea House Publishers, 2002.

Crewe, Sabrina. *Lexington and Concord*. Milwaukee: Gareth Stevens Publishing, 2004.

Jarrett-Silox, Diane. *Heroines of the American Revolution: America's Founding Mothers*. Chapel Hill, N.C.: Green Angel Press, 1998.

Todd, Anne. *The Revolutionary War*. Mankato, Minn.: Capstone Press, 2001.

WEBSITES
Cumberland County Historical Society
www.historicalsociety.com/vmt.html

Historic Valley Forge
www.ushistory.org/valleyforge/index.html

Kid Info: The American Revolution
www.kidinfo.com/American_History/American_Revolution.html

Molly Pitcher
www.earlyamerica.com/molly_pitcher.html

PBS: The American Revolution
www.pbs.org/ktca/liberty

Virtual Marching Tour of the American Revolution
www.ushistory.org/march

Index

Index

page:

4: © Bettmann/CORBIS

7: © Bettmann/CORBIS

14: © Bettmann/CORBIS

16: © Historical Picture Archive/
CORBIS

31: © Art Resource, NY

36: © Carl and Ann Purcell/CORBIS

49: © Bettmann/CORBIS

54: © National Portrait Gallery,
Smithsonian Institution/
Art Resource, NY

57: © Bob Krist/CORBIS

64: © John Springer/
CORBIS

75: © Bettmann/CORBIS

84: © Bettmann/CORBIS

94: © Bettmann/CORBIS

96: © Bettmann/CORBIS

103: © Joseph Sohm;
ChromoSohm Inc./
CORBIS

104: © Lucien Aigner/CORBIS

Cover: © Bettmann/CORBIS

RACHEL A. KOESTLER-GRACK has worked with nonfiction books as an editor and writer since 1999. She lives on a farm near Glencoe, Minnesota. During her career, she has worked extensively in several different historical periods, including the colonial era, the Civil War era, the Great Depression, and the civil rights movement.

DEC 1 4 2005

DEMCO